The End of – Well, Pretty Much Everything

Walking into Eternity

Book Ten

Walking with Jesus

Becoming the Best Me I Can Be

Pamela D White

All scripture quotations, unless otherwise indicated, are taken from the Holy Bible, **New King James Version©**. Copyright © 1982 by Thomas Nelson, Inc. Used by permission. All rights reserved.

Scripture quotations marked NIV are taken from the Holy Bible, **New International Version** ®, NIV ®. Copyright © 1973, 1978, 1984 by **Biblica, Inc.® Used by permission. All rights reserved worldwide.**

Scripture quotations marked NASB are taken from the Holy Bible, **New American Standard Bible®**, Copyright © 1960, 1971, 1977, 1995, 2020 by The Lockman Foundation. All rights reserved.

Scripture quotations marked AMP are taken from the Holy Bible, **Amplified**, copyright © 2015 by The Lockman Foundation, La Habra, CA 90631. All rights reserved. For Permission to Quote information visit http://www.lockman.org/

Scripture quotations marked ESV are taken from the ESV® Bible (The Holy Bible, **English Standard Version®**). ESV® Text Edition: 2016. Copyright © 2001 by Crossway, a publishing ministry of Good News Publishers. The ESV® text has been reproduced in cooperation with and by permission of Good News Publishers. Unauthorized reproduction of this publication is prohibited. All rights reserved.

Scripture quotations marked NLT are taken from the Holy Bible, **New Living Translation,** copyright © 1996, 2004, 2015 by Tyndale House Foundation. Used by permission of Tyndale House Publishers, Inc., Carol Stream, Illinois 60188. All rights reserved.

Scripture quotations marked MSG are taken from **THE MESSAGE**, copyright © 1993, 2002, 2018 by Eugene H. Peterson. Used by permission of NavPress. All rights reserved. Represented by Tyndale House Publishers, Inc.

Scripture quotations marked AKJV are taken from the Holy Bible, **Authorized King James Version**, The Authorized (King James) Version of the Bible ('the KJV'), the rights in which are vested in the Crown in the United Kingdom, is reproduced here by permission of the Crown's patentee, Cambridge University Press. The Cambridge KJV text, including paragraphing, is reproduced here by permission of Cambridge University Press.

A publication of Blooming Desert Ministries

ISBN 978-1-7370803-8-1 (sc print)
ISBN 978-1-7370803-9-8 (ebook)

Printed in the United States of America
Copyright © 2021 by Pamela D White
All Rights Reserved.

IngramSparks Publishing (Ingram: Lightning Source, LLC)

One Ingram Blvd., La Vergne, TN 37086

Publishing Note: Publishing style capitalizes certain pronouns in Scriptures that refer to the Father, Son, and Holy Spirit, and may differ from other publishing styles. **All emphasis in the Scriptures' quotations is the authors.** The name satan and related names are not capitalized as the author's preference not to acknowledge him, even though it violates grammatical rules.

No part of this book may be reproduced or transmitted in any form or by any means, electronic or mechanical – including photocopying, recording, or by any information storage and retrieval system – without permission in writing from the publisher. Please direct inquires to PDW Publications.

Dedication

This book series is dedicated to you.

Everyone has opportunities to become a better version of themselves. My prayer is that this book series helps you on that journey. The Lord loves you so much He desires an intimate relationship with you. You are special to Him and He loves spending time with you. Walking and talking with Jesus every day should be the norm, not the exception. Life can bring difficult circumstances and situations. When you walk with Jesus, life events, are not only manageable but can be turned for your good.

"And we know that all things work together for good to those who love God, to those who are the called according to His purpose," Romans 8:28.

Come with me into this exploration of how you can develop a relationship with Jesus and walk with Him every day. This is an opportunity to become a better you.

Acknowledgments

The Great Commission given by our Lord and Savior Jesus Christ noted in Matthew 28:16-20 is my inspiration for this publication. Verses 19-20 state, *"Go therefore and make disciples of all the nations, baptizing them in the name of the Father and of the Son and of the Holy Spirit, teaching them to observe all things that I have commanded you; and lo, I am with you always, even to the end of the age."* This verse is the very basis for missionary work all over the globe. I have been blessed to be able to serve in a few of those missions. Missions are an amazing experience. I came to realize though that everyone cannot always do all the parts commanded in these verses. I can't always go. I didn't often get to baptize. What I realized was that I can do my part in teaching to observes the truths of the Scriptures. My desire to fulfill the teaching part of the Great Commission was the inspiration for this work. My pastor, Bishop Larry Taylor, and First Lady Desetra Taylor allowed our church to use these Bible studies in our New Life Discipleship classes for nearly twenty years. The work has also been used in prison ministries in central Illinois for as many years. The teaching has proven effective in changing many lives and discipling the children of God. Thank you, Bishop and First Lady, for teaching a balanced spiritual and natural life so I could complete this project and see the impact of the work on people's lives.

Bishop positioned me to be the director of New Life Ministries Discipleship for several years. New Life classes were designed to teach those new to Christianity or new to the church the foundational truths needed to build a solid life in Christ. During that time, this work was fine-tuned with the help and input from the dedicated, gifted, and anointed New Life teachers Minister Retta Smith, Minister James Smith, Minister Debby Henkel, Dr. Terry Husband, Minister Char-Michelle McDowell, Minister Yvonne Smith, Minister Herbert Smyer, and Professor Susan Gibson along with the encouragement and guidance of Dr. Chequita Brown and community service advocate Minister Patricia Turner. I also want to give a shout-out to Dr. Wanda Turner, nationally acclaimed minister, teacher, prophet, life coach, mentor, and best-selling author, who continued to encourage me to just publish the thing! Thanks to all of you. Each of you has made a significant impact on my life.

My dear friend and mentor, First Lady Marshell Wickware, supported the project and pushed me to publish it for years. Thanks for not giving up on me!

My life-long friend, Robin McClallen, thank you for all your support, input, and encouraging me to publish something. You have been instrumental in making me an author.

A special thanks to my husband, Brian K. White, for his patience and prayers as I spent hours and hours researching, writing, and rewriting. Thanks, BW!

Most of all thank you to the Holy Spirit and my Lord and Savior Jesus Christ. I present this work in obedience and honor to You.

Contents

Introduction	11
The Seven Dispensations	13
Rapture of Believers	17
Judgment Seat of Christ (Bema)	21
The Tribulation	27
Elements of the Tribulation	29
Marriage Feast of the Lamb	31
Battle of Armageddon	33
Second Coming of Christ	35
The Millennium	37
Final Rebellion	39
White Throne Judgment	41
New Kingdom	45
Why do I Need to Know About the All This?	49
Stepping Stones	51
The End of – Well, Pretty Much Everything	53
Glossary	55
About the Author	61

Book Ten

The End of – Well, Pretty Much Everything
Walking in Eternity

OBJECTIVE

This chapter presents the doctrine of the end times. We will present an overview of the Biblical study of end times prophecy and the events of the last days. Also, we will discuss death, the Last Judgment, heaven, hell, and the ultimate destiny of humankind.

MEMORY VERSE

"And I saw heaven opened, and behold a white horse; and he that sat on him was called Faithful and True, and in righteousness he does judge and make war... And he has on his clothing and on his thigh a name written, King of kings, and Lord of lords," Revelation 19:11 & 16 AKJV.

The End of – Well, Pretty Much Everything
Walking in Eternity

A. Seven Dispensations

B. The Rapture of Believers

C. Judgment Seat of Christ

D. Tribulation

E. Marriage Feast of the Lamb

F. Battle of Armageddon

G. Second Coming of Christ

H. Millennium

I. Final Rebellion

J. White Throne Judgment

K. New Kingdom

The End of – Well, Pretty Much Everything
Walking in Eternity
Introduction

The sky is falling! The sky is falling! Chicken Little and all her friends, Henny Penny, Goosy Loosey, and Turkey Lurkey went searching for the King to let him know there was chaos in the world and surely the end was near. All you have to do is watch the news on any day and you will see the world you live in is also in chaos - earthquakes, tornados, hurricanes, tsunamis, fires, floods, and drought just for starters. The level of wickedness has escalated and become more obvious with child abductions, human trafficking, serial killers, bombers, abusers, users, terrorists and so much more. Every time I see these things in the news, I am like Chicken Little running to my King.

Jesus Christ is the King of everything. He knows exactly what is going on. God even warned you about it in His Word. He provided descriptions of many of the things that would happen, as the end of time grew closer. This book explores the events of the end of time. Remember, God created time when He made the sun, moon, and stars, setting seasons and time into being. Time will eventually end. We are going to look at a few things the Bible tells us about the end of time. Academia calls it eschatology. The word eschatology is derived from the Greek words eschatos, which means the last things, and logos, which means the study of. Therefore, eschatology deals with the study of the final events in the history of the world and the end times. These events include the rapture, the second coming of Christ, the tribulation, the millennial kingdom, and judgment. The end of the age is not something to fear when living with Christ as your Savior. The account of the end of time is a call to evangelism to provide friends and loved ones with an opportunity to choose the Way of Christ for their life. It is also a call to walk holy and circumspectly before God at all times since you do not know the day or hour that events will occur.

"And when these things begin to come to pass, then look up, and lift up your heads; for your redemption draws near," Luke 21:28 AKJV.

The Seven Dispensations

To better see that time is coming to a close, the Bible provides an excellent timeline painting a picture of the periods of time through history. The Scriptures divide periods of time from Genesis to Revelation into seven unequal periods, which Christian scholars have termed as dispensations. These periods are sometimes called 'the ages' as in Ephesians 2:7 *"That in the ages to come he might show the exceeding riches of his grace in his kindness toward us through Christ Jesus,"* AKJV. Another reference for the last days found in Scripture is the term *"day of the Lord."*

Each period represents a change in the method God deals with humankind regarding teaching man his responsibility as a servant of God, preparing man for the coming of Jesus Christ, and developing man for his role in eternity. You have a disadvantage of being on earth as a human. You cannot see the big picture of what God is doing and has been doing throughout the ages. Remember the movie Miracle on 34th Street? Little Susan Walker was in her high-rise apartment watching the Thanksgiving Day Parade. From her high viewpoint, she could see the parade from the first police car to Santa's sleigh at the end. The people on the street could only see part of the parade directly in front of them. Susan's vantage point offered her the full picture. As a resident of earth, you are much like the people on the street at the parade and can only see those things close to you. God has the vantage point of all creation from start to finish as Susan did with the parade. He can see time from its beginning to its end and everything in between. I heard a Bible teacher describe time more like a belt. He put the two ends together just as it would be around your waist and described time as circular with God in the middle looking at all of time from beginning to end. Either example shows that God sees it all and He has given you a picture of time in the seven dispensations or ages of the Bible. Within each dispensation, there is a new learning experience, an opportunity to grow that comes when mankind finds he cannot fulfill the responsibility on his own, and the promise God offers as man moves to the next phase of development. The development of humankind is much like the development of a child. Man begins in innocence and learns through various experiences about how much Father God loves and cares for him, how to live with others, and how to succeed.

The seven dispensations are:

1. The Age of Innocence—Man started innocent but fell to evil. Genesis 1-3.

2. The Age of Conscience—Man understands there is a right and a wrong. Genesis 4.

3. The Age of Human Government—Man grows in his understanding that he has authority and must use it to rule the earth. Genesis 8:15; 9:1-6

4. The Age of Promise—God gives man promises and makes a covenant with His people. Genesis 12:1-3.

5. The Age of Law—God gives man the law to help man understand his need for salvation. Book of Exodus through Matthew 3.

6. The Age of Grace—Jesus arrives to bring salvation and grace. New Testament to today.

7. The Age of Kingdom—Jesus returns in majesty, the final judgment takes place, and time ceases as humankind moves into eternity. Not here yet, but it's coming!

Walking with Jesus - Series

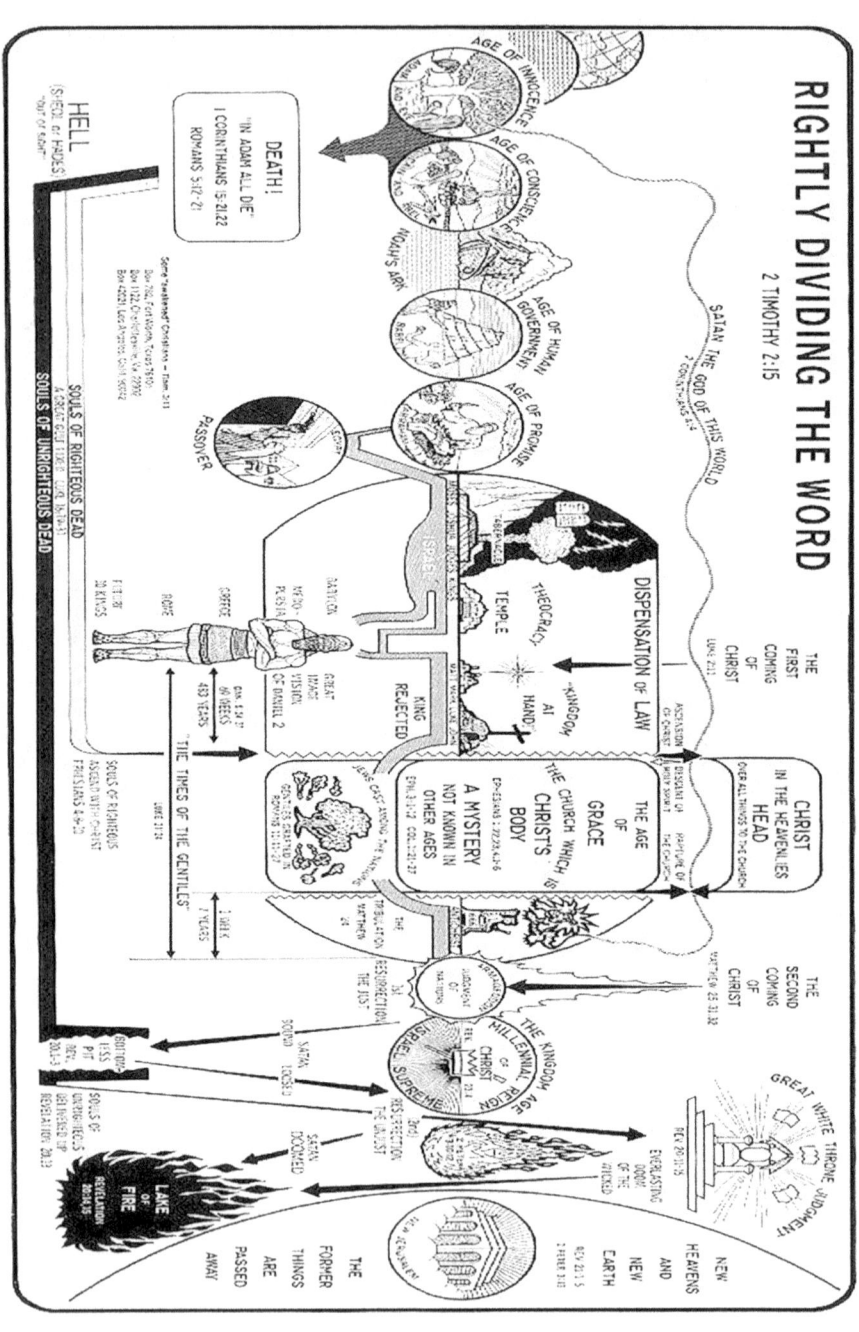

Chart by Charles Larkin

Rapture of Believers

Did you notice from the list or the chart that we are currently in the Sixth Dispensation? As we come to the end of the Sixth Dispensation and enter the Seventh and last dispensation, there are a series of events that occur, beginning with an event known as the Rapture. The term rapture is not found in the Bible but is firmly based on Scripture. The term used in the Scripture comes from the Hebrew word *harpazo*, which means to 'snatch away' or to be 'caught up.' Jesus descends from heaven with a shout and the trump of God to gather His people and take them out of the earth before the tribulation begins in full force. When talking about the last days we often think of the book of Revelation, which is a prophetic book about events occurring in the end. However, there are references throughout Scripture about these events. Here are a few of the scriptures describing the snatching away of believers.

1 Thessalonians 4:15-17 describes the **SNATCHING AWAY** of believers like this: *"For this we say to you by the word of the Lord, that we which are alive and remain to the coming of the Lord shall not prevent them which are asleep. For the Lord himself shall descend from heaven with a shout, with the voice of the archangel, and with the trump of God: and the dead in Christ shall rise first: Then we which are alive and remain shall be caught up togeth-*

er with them in the clouds, to meet the Lord in the air: and so shall we ever be with the Lord," KJV.

1 Corinthians 15:51-55 exposes the mystery of Jesus snatching His people. *"Behold, I tell you a mystery: We shall not all sleep, but we shall all be changed—in a moment, in the twinkling of an eye, at the last trumpet. For the trumpet will sound, and the dead will be raised incorruptible, and we shall be changed. For this corruptible must put on incorruption, and this mortal must put on immortality. So when this corruptible has put on incorruption, and this mortal has put on immortality, then shall be brought to pass the saying that is written: "Death is swallowed up in victory. O Death, where is your sting? O Hades, where is your victory?"*

The Lord loves you and has no desire for you to endure the tribulations that are coming. 1 Thessalonians 1:10 lets you know Jesus is coming to deliver you from the wrath that will be unleashed on the enemies of God. *"And to wait for His Son from heaven, whom He raised from the dead, even Jesus who delivers us from the wrath to come."*

1 Thessalonians 2:19 refers to Jesus coming for you. *"For what is our hope, or joy, or crown of rejoicing? Is it not even you in the presence of our Lord Jesus Christ at His coming?"*

The Lord loves you. He does not want you to be on earth to endure the devastation and terror that is coming. Jesus is coming for all of His children that remain on the earth when the Seventh Dispensation begins.

There are other ideas about when the rapture occurs. Some teach the rapture occurs in the middle of the tribulation and others teach it occurs at the end of the tribulation. I encourage you to search the scriptures for yourself and come to your own conclusion. Some say when the rapture occurs is not important, but frankly, I don't want to be here during that time, nor do I want my family and friends to endure it. God is love and I believe the Scripture shows that He loves me too much to have me go through the tribulation when I have given Him my life.

Judgment Seat of Christ (Bema)

When a Christian leaves earth and steps into eternity with Christ, the next step is to appear before the Judgment Seat of Christ. This is called the Bema Seat. The term Bema Seat comes from the ancient Olympics. A judge would sit on a seat at the finish line to decide who placed in a race. The Greeks called this place of judgment the Bema Seat. It was a seat of verdicts and rewards as they judged the runners according to their placing. The Judgment Seat or Bema Seat of Christ offers the same judgment. The Olympic Bema Seat did not determine if the runners were in the race. They were already runners. The Bema Seat did not determine if someone finished the race. The runners had crossed the finish line. A Bema Seat judge determined the reward each person received for their race. The Judgment Seat of Christ is also a place of reward. It doesn't determine your salvation. If you didn't have salvation, you would never even see the Judgment Seat. You joined the race. You ran the race, then you finished the race. Now comes your rewards.

Christians or born-again believers before the Judgment Seat receive an evaluation for the works they have done, including both good and bad.

The Bema Judgment distributes awards to the saints for their work. It isn't your occupation on earth that is judged. It is the work of your heart. 2 Corinthians 5:10 states, *"For we must all appear before the judgment seat of Christ; that every one may receive the things done in his body, according to that he has done, whether it be good or bad,"* AKJV.

Again, the Judgment Seat does not judge salvation. That decision is made when you accept Jesus Christ as your Lord. The Judgment Seat is the place where your works are tried by fire. 1 Corinthians 3:11-15 explains,

"For no other foundation can anyone lay than that which is laid, which is Jesus Christ. Now if anyone builds on this foundation with gold, silver, precious stones, wood, hay, straw, each one's work will become clear; for the Day will declare it, because it will be revealed by fire; and the fire will test each one's work, of what sort it is. If anyone's work which he has built on it endures, he will receive a reward. If anyone's work is burned, he will suffer loss; but he himself will be saved, yet so as through fire."

Every Christian will appear before the Judgment Seat of Christ. No one is exempt. It is a time of accountability. Keep in mind that God knows everyone sometimes makes bad choices. That is why He gives you the amazing gift of forgiveness. Anything you have placed under the blood of Jesus through forgiveness is gone. The Bible says in Psalms 103:12 that it is removed as far as the east is from the west which is unmeasurable. In other words, it no longer exists. No worries. All your bad decisions from your entire life are not on display. When you accept the forgiveness of God for any bad decisions, they are gone. This is why it is important to pray as David did in Psalm 51:10 *"Create in me a clean heart, O God, and renew a right spirit in me"* ESV. Once the Lord judges your works, rewards are presented in the form of heavenly treasure, fulfilled promises, commendations, and crowns. Here are a few of the crowns the Bible mentions and the scripture that describes the crown:

- Incorruptible Crown—1 Corinthians 9:24-26 *"Do you not know that those who run in a race all run, but one receives the prize? Run in such a way that you may obtain it. And everyone who competes for the prize is temperate in all things. Now they do it to obtain a perishable crown, but we for an imperishable crown. Therefore I run thus: not with uncertainty. Thus I fight: not as one who beats the air."*

For those who run the race of life and fight the good fight of faith on their journey.

- Victor's Crown—2 Timothy 2:1-13 v.4 & 5 *"No one engaged in warfare entangles himself with the affairs of this life, that he may please him who enlisted him as a soldier. And also if anyone competes in athletics, he is not crowned unless he competes according to the rules."*

For those who fight to win regarding righteousness.

- Crown of Life—Revelations 2:10 *"Do not fear any of those things which you are about to suffer. Indeed, the devil is about to throw some of you into prison, that you may be tested, and you will have tribulation ten days. Be faithful until death, and I will give you the crown of life."*

For those who endure trials, tribulations, struggle, hardships, etc and remain faithful.

- Crown of Glory—1 Peter 5:2-4 *"Shepherd the flock of God which is among you, serving as overseers, not by compulsion but willingly, not for dishonest gain but eagerly; nor as being lords over those entrusted to you, but being examples to the flock; and when the Chief Shepherd appears, you will receive the crown of glory that does not fade away."*

Also known as the pastor's crown and is for those who give their lives to teaching the Word of God which could include preachers, teachers, missionaries, evangelists, etc.

- Crown of Righteousness—2 Timothy 4:6-8 *"For I am already being poured out as a drink offering, and the time of my departure is at hand. I have fought the good fight, I have finished the race, I have kept the faith. Finally, there is laid up for me the crown of righteousness, which the Lord, the righteous Judge, will give to me on that Day, and not to me only but also to all who have loved His appearing."*

A special crown for those who live a righteous and holy life For those who love the Lord's appearing.

- Crown of Rejoicing—1 Thessalonians 2:19-20 *"For what is our hope, or joy, or crown of rejoicing? Is it not even you in the presence of our Lord Jesus Christ at His coming? For you are our glory and joy."*

Soul Winner's crown for those who devote their time to winning souls.

There are many rewards noted throughout Scripture. Here are a few verses that describe some promised rewards. I encourage you to take some time to search out these scriptures and look for more.

The End of – Well, Pretty Much Everything

Romans 14:10-11

1 Corinthians 15:10

2 Corinthians 3:11-15

1 John 2:28

Revelations 3:11-12

Revelations 22:12

Revelations 16

Revelations 19

Zechariah 14

Matthew 6:20

1 Peter 1:4

Matthew 25:21

Luke 19:17

1 Corinthians 4:5

Revelations 2:7, 11, 17, 26

The Tribulation

While the saints of God are standing before the Judgment Seat of Christ having their works judged, down on earth is chaos and turmoil. Tribulation is occurring all over the world. The tribulation is seven years where those who are left behind during the rapture experience a series of hardships and disasters. First, everyone left on earth is wondering where all the people went! Was it aliens? The zombie apocalypse? Some kind of terrorist mass abduction or genocide? Can you imagine the confusion and chaos as millions of people disappear from the earth when the rapture occurs? Then the grace of God we have been living under lifts and the wrath of God is unleashed on sin.

Here's a little of what the tribulation looks like. Revelation 6:14-17 *"Then the sky receded as a scroll when it is rolled up, and every mountain and island was moved out of its place. And the kings of the earth, the great men, the rich men, the commanders, the mighty men, every slave and every free man, hid themselves in the caves and in the rocks of the mountains, and said to the mountains and rocks, "Fall on us and hide us from the face of Him who sits on the throne and from the wrath of the Lamb! For the great day of His wrath has come, and who is able to stand?"*

You do not want to be on earth during the tribulation. The tribulation is also known as the Day of the Lord (Isaiah 2:12) and the day of trouble (Daniel 12:1). All of God's people are gone. The Holy Spirit's presence that lived in God's people left with them. This leaves those left behind to delve into decadence and depravity. Selfishness will be at an all-time high. Because of such brazen depravity, the age of grace ends, and the wrath of God is poured out on the earth. This is also the time of the wrath of satan and his demons and the time of the wrath of man. Matthew 24:12-14 gives a brief description, *"And because iniquity shall abound, the love of many shall wax cold. But he that shall endure unto the end, the same shall be saved. And this gospel of the kingdom shall be preached in all the world for a witness unto all nations; and then shall the end come,"* KJV.

The people left behind on earth, those who refuse Christ as their Savior will have an opportunity to change their minds and accept the gift of salvation. It won't be easy, but it won't be impossible. Revelation 9:1-11 is one scripture passage that describes the elements of tribulation. We will not discuss each element, as there is so much. I encourage you to read the very picturesque description in the book of Revelation.

Elements of the Tribulation

Seven Seals

White horse—conquering power

Red horse—war & bloodshed

Black horse—famine

Pale horse—Pestilence & death

Souls under the altar martyred

Great earthquake

Golden sensor

Seven Trumpets

Hail, fire, blood

Burning mountain

Wormwood

Sun diminished

Plague of locust

Sea turns to blood

Christ rules

Seven Key Figures

Woman—Israel

Dragon—Satan

Male child—Christ

Michael—the Archangel

Remnant—saved Israel

Antichrist—beast out of the sea

False Prophet—beast out of the earth

Seven Bowls

Boils

Plague of horsemen

Darkness

Euphrates dried up

Hail

- Rivers turn to blood
- Great heat
- Seven Dooms of Babylon
- Devoid of human life
- Burned with fire
- Destroyed in one hour

- Seven Dooms of Babylon
- People afraid to enter her borders
- Riches brought to nothing
- Violently overthrown
- All activity ceases

Marriage Feast of the Lamb

(Marriage Supper of the Lamb)

While all of those horrendous things are taking place on earth, the saints in heaven are having a huge feast. After the saints of God have come before the Bema Judgment Seat, they are invited into the great banqueting hall of the King of Kings. Here they will join in a celebration with their Great King and Redeemer to celebrate the marriage of the Lamb of God or Jesus Christ. So, who is the one who will be the bride of Jesus? You! Christians. People who believe Christ is their Savior. The church. Together, the people of God are the bride of Christ. Isaiah 54:5 states, *"For your Maker is your husband, the Lord of hosts is His name; and your Redeemer is the Holy One of Israel; He is called the God of the whole earth."*

It may seem strange that men and women will be the bride or that multiple people are considered the bride. Maybe it is easier to think of the bride as the Church. Not a church building, but the people who are the children of God and who love the Lord. A magnificent celebration will take place as this wedding takes place. It will be a great time of rejoicing and blessing. Revelation 19:7-10 *"Let us be glad and rejoice, and give honor to him: for the marriage of the Lamb is come, and his wife has made herself ready. And to her was granted that she should be arrayed in fine linen, clean and white: for the fine linen is the righteousness of saints. And he said to me, Write, Blessed are they which are called to the marriage supper of the Lamb. And he said to me, These are the true sayings of God. And I fell at his feet to worship him,"* AKJV.

Battle of Armageddon

Now let's look at what is happening back on earth while this wedding celebration is occurring. The armies of the antichrist, all the combined armies of the nations, are in a fight to the death. Armageddon comes from the Hebrew word *Har-megadon* which means Mount Megiddo. Sometimes, we call this 'That Great Day of God Almighty.' Revelation 16:14-16 describes the Battle of Armageddon, *"For they are the spirits of devils, working miracles, which go forth to the kings of the earth and of the whole world, to gather them to the battle of that great day of God Almighty. Behold, I come as a thief. Blessed is he that watches, and keeps his garments, lest he walk naked, and they see his shame. And he gathered them together into a place called in the Hebrew tongue Armageddon,"* AKJV.

The battle begins when the enemy has gathered his ten-kingdom empire. This huge empire and a picture of the battle are recorded in Daniel 11: 4-11. There are agreements, treaties, dominions, kings of north & south & east conspiring against one another in great rage. The battle will be immediately after the seven-year tribulation. The world has already gone through much destruction and devastation during those seven years. Millions have died. Now the final battle takes place. It is a war over power and territory. The war includes the struggle for power over the Holy Land including Jerusalem. Jesus Christ returns to earth to fight this final conflict against the forces of evil.

"For as the lightning comes out of the east, and shines even to the west; so shall also the coming of the Son of man be. For wherever the carcass is, there will the eagles be gathered together. Immediately after the tribulation of those days shall the sun be darkened, and the moon shall not give her light, and the stars shall fall from heaven, and the powers of the heavens shall be shaken," Matthew 24:27-31 AKJV.

The **BATTLE OF ARMAGEDDON** has multiple purposes. These are a few of those purposes and the scripture supporting those purposes.

- Deliver Israel from the Antichrist - *Zechariah 14*

- Punish nations for the persecution of the Jews - *Matthew 25:31-46*

- Set up the new kingdom – *Daniel 7:13-14*

- To rid the earth of rebellion - *1 Corinthians 15:24-29*

- To establish the eternal perfect state – *Revelation 21:2, 22:5*

Second Coming of Christ

During the Battle of Armageddon, Jesus returns to earth to lead His saints in a battle against the forces of evil. The Second Coming is different from the rapture. During the rapture, Christ came in the clouds to remove His people from the earth. In the Second Coming, He descends to earth to bring evil its ultimate defeat and establish His reign. Jesus does not come alone. His army is with Him in great strength. The army includes angelic beings and God's saints, the armies of heaven. Revelation 19:11 & 14 paint a picture of how this army descends; *"Now I saw heaven opened, and behold, a white horse. And He who sat on him was called Faithful and True, and in righteousness He judges and makes war… And the armies in heaven, clothed in fine linen, white and clean, followed Him on white horses"*. Christ comes to judge and make war with the Antichrist and the armies of the earth. He also came to earth to establish His kingdom. This era will end when Jesus destroys the armies of the earth; the false prophet and the antichrist are bound for **1,000 YEARS**.

"For certain men have crept in unnoticed, who long ago were marked out for this condemnation, ungodly men, who turn the grace of our God into lewdness and deny the only Lord God and our Lord Jesus Christ," Jude 1:4.

The Millennium

The armies of the earth are destroyed and the false prophets are gone. The antichrist is dead. Satan and his demons are bound for a thousand years, called the millennium. The millennium is a thousand years of peace. Christ is reigning and Satan is bound. Imagine life without depression, sickness, lies, fear, worry, and doubt. There is no pain, abuse, hatred, or anything the enemy used to assault people with.

"Then I saw an angel coming down from heaven, having the key to the bottomless pit and a great chain in his hand. He laid hold of the dragon, that serpent of old, who is the Devil and Satan, and bound him for a thousand years; and he cast him into the bottomless pit, and shut him up, and set a seal on him, so that he should deceive the nations no more till the thousand years were finished. But after these things he must be released for a little while. And I saw thrones, and they sat on them, and judgment was committed to them. Then I saw the souls of those who had been beheaded for their witness to Jesus and for the word of God, who had not worshiped the beast or his image, and had not received his mark on their foreheads or on their hands. And they lived and reigned with Christ for a thousand years. But the rest of the dead did not live again until the thousand years were finished. This is the first resurrection. Blessed and holy is he who has part in the first resurrection.

Over such the second death has no power, but they shall be priests of God and of Christ, and shall reign with Him a thousand years," Revelation 20:1-6.

Christ rules and reigns on the earth for a thousand years. There will be great **PEACE, JOY, HOLINESS, TRUTH,** and knowledge of God.

"When the Son of man shall come in his glory, and all the holy angels with him, then shall he sit on the throne of his glory," Matthew 25:31 KJV.

Final Rebellion

After a thousand years of peace, Satan is released for one last showdown. The final rebellion is called the Battle of Gog and Magog. Satan is loosed and deceives the nations and leads one final revolt against Christ. The number of people that side with Satan is as many as the number of the sand of the sea, an innumerable group of deceived people. The enemy surrounds God's city and the saints of God. God in His majesty and splendor sends fire down from heaven and devours the enemy.

Revelation 20:7-10 describes this event. *"Now when the thousand years have expired, Satan will be released from his prison and will go out to deceive the nations which are in the four corners of the earth, Gog and Magog, to gather them together to battle, whose number is as the sand of the sea. They went up on the breadth of the earth and surrounded the camp of the saints and the beloved city. And fire came down from God out of heaven and devoured them. The devil, who deceived them, was cast into the lake of fire and brimstone where the beast and the false prophet are. And they will be tormented day and night forever and ever."*

As noted in this scripture, God then cast Satan in the lake of fire and brimstone. His torment lasts forever and ever, day and night, ceaseless.

White Throne Judgment

Earlier we talked about the Judgment Seat of Christ, where the works of the saints of God are judged and the saints are held accountable for their choices. Back on the earth, there are hundreds of thousands of people left behind enduring the tribulation. During the time of the tribulation, some individuals realize the truth of Jesus Christ and become believers in the birth, death, resurrection, and forgiveness of sins that Jesus brought to humanity. Others remain deceived by Satan. The final battle has occurred and Christ and His army are confirmed victorious. Satan, the beast, and his cohorts have been cast into the lake of fire. All those people who died during the tribulation, the wars, and the final battle now must face Christ and be judged. The White Throne Judgment is not for the saints of God who died before the tribulation or for those taken to heaven in the rapture. The White Throne Judgment is for everyone who was not in attendance at the Bema Judgment Seat of Christ. It is at the White Throne Judgment Seat that the book of life is opened. This book records everyone's deeds throughout their entire life. Each deed, decision, thought, and intent comes under judgment. Remember that God gives everyone an opportunity for forgiveness. Those who refuse forgiveness and restoration of their relationship with the Lord are judged at this time. Rewards and punishment are granted. It won't be pretty. In Matthew 13:42, Jesus describes wailing and gnashing of teeth. He also says the righteous will shine like the sun. Choose wisely, grasshopper.

"Then I saw a great white throne and Him who sat on it, from whose face the earth and the heaven fled away. And there was found no place for them. And I saw the dead, small and great, standing before God, and books were opened. And another book was opened, which is the Book of Life. And the dead were judged according to their works, by the things which were written in the books. The sea gave up the dead who were in it, and Death and Hades delivered up the dead who were in them. And they were judged, each one according to his works. Then Death and Hades were cast into the lake of fire. This is the second death. And anyone not found written in the Book of Life was cast into the lake of fire," Revelation 20:11-15.

The second death described in Revelation 20 is why you want to make sure you and those you love understand the truth of Christ. You do not want to suffer a second death. Jesus tells a parable in Luke showing the difficulty of choosing the way of Christ if you give in to your sinful nature and selfish ways.

"Strive to enter through the narrow gate, for many, I say to you, will seek to enter and will not be able. When once the Master of the house has risen up and shut the door, and you begin to stand outside and knock at the door, saying, 'Lord, Lord, open for us,' and He will answer and say to you, 'I do not know you, where you are from,' then you will begin to say, 'We ate and drank in Your presence, and You taught in our streets.' But He will say, 'I tell you I do not know you, where you are from. Depart from Me, all you workers of iniquity.' There will be weeping and gnashing of teeth, when you see Abraham and Isaac and Jacob and all the prophets in the kingdom of God, and your-

selves thrust out. They will come from the east and the west, from the north and the south, and sit down in the kingdom of God. And indeed there are last who will be first, and there are first who will be last," Luke 13:24-30.

The scriptures remind you from Genesis to Revelation, watch yourself, love God, and love people. Living forever in eternal blessing, not punishment and the second death, is your choice.

New Kingdom

Now all the ages are full or completed. Every prophecy has been fulfilled. Every single person who ever lived had the opportunity to receive Jesus into his or her life. The final war is over. The New Kingdom is established. It is here the victors of the greatest of all wars dwell with Christ in their new glorified bodies. Full fellowship with God is restored and a world far better than Eden exists. There is no sickness, suffering, evil, or death. The people who enjoy the new kingdom are those who did not suffer the second death. The Apostle John had a vision of the new heaven and the new earth that makes up the New Kingdom, which he recorded in the book of Revelation. I encourage you to read the entirety of Revelation 21 for an amazing picture of the glory of the Lord, the streets of pure gold transparent as glass, the foundation of precious stones, gates of pearl, and no one is crying from pain or sorrow. It's magnificent and is the new home of the bride of Christ.

"Now I saw a new heaven and a new earth, for the first heaven and the first earth had passed away. Also there was no more sea. Then I, John, saw the holy city, New Jerusalem, coming down out of heaven from God, prepared as a bride adorned for her husband… And he carried me away in the Spirit to a great and high mountain, and showed me the great city, the holy Jerusalem, descending out of heaven from God," Revelation 21:1-2, 10.

The Old Testament also talks about the new heavens and new earth. It is so magnificent that you won't even remember the old that no longer exists.

"For, behold, I create new heavens and a new earth: and the former shall not be remembered, nor come into mind," Isaiah 65:17 KJV.

God created the new heaven and the new earth just for you, the believer, the child of God, the apple of God's eye, His bride to live in forever with Christ.

"For as the new heavens and the new earth, which I will make, shall remain before me, said the Lord, so shall your seed and your name remain," Isaiah 66:22 KJV.

The Bible is full of many details to expect during this time of tribulation, final wars, and the entrance of a new world. We have barely skimmed the surface of the end times in this chapter. The Lord wants you to know what's coming and has given you tools to prepare. He gave you His Word so you have direction in your life and would know how much He loves you and wants to spend eternity with you. He gave you instructions on how to bring others along with you into the New Kingdom as the bride of Christ. He desires that you spend all eternity with Him. Jesus died so you would be free from sin. He gave you gifts, so you could help others make that same decision. God gave you the Holy Spirit to give you the power and authority to assist you while you live in a fallen world. He showed you the way to spend forever with Him. You might live on earth right now, but this is not your true home. You are an ambassador for Christ, here to stomp on the enemy's head and lead others to the truth. Paul says it best in 1 Corinthians 5:11-21. We will end this chapter with part of that passage:

"Because we understand our fearful responsibility to the Lord, we work hard to persuade others. God knows we are sincere, and I hope you know this, too… And all of this is a gift from God, who brought us back to himself through Christ. And God has given us this task of reconciling people to him. For God was in Christ, reconciling the world to himself, no longer counting people's sins against them. And he gave us this wonderful message of reconciliation. So we are Christ's ambassadors; God is making his appeal through us. We speak for Christ when we plead, "Come back to God!" For God made Christ, who never sinned, to be the offering for our sin, so that we could be made right with God through Christ."

Come, Lord Jesus!

Why do I Need to Know About the All This?

Good question. Thanks for asking. We talk about the End Times because the Word instructs every believer to get ready. No one knows when Jesus is returning. Not even Jesus knows. Only the Father knows when the Son is returning to earth. Jesus told his disciples, *"Heaven and earth will pass away, but My words will by no means pass away. But of that day and hour no one knows, not even the angels of heaven, but My Father only. But as the days of Noah were, so also will the coming of the Son of Man be,"* Matthew 24:35-37 (Also found in Mark 13:32 and Acts 1:7). You could turn around in the next instant and be snatched away to be with the Lord or left behind if you are not ready.

The Word instructs believers to be vigilant. You are also instructed to be diligent in the Word for you and your children and your grandchildren. Since you don't know when Jesus is returning, everyone needs to be presented with the Gospel and taught the Word of God so they will be ready, too.

"Only take heed to yourself, and diligently keep yourself, lest you forget the things your eyes have seen, and lest they depart from your heart all the

days of your life. And teach them to your children and your grandchildren," Deuteronomy 4:9.

Peter, John, and Paul all give clear directions on how to be vigilant and diligently make yourself and others ready. His instructions are to practice holiness and do good to others at every opportunity. You are to work the works of God at all times because the Day of the Lord will come before you realize it and you want to be found ready and doing the Lord's work.

"But the day of the Lord will come as a thief in the night, in which the heavens will pass away with a great noise, and the elements will melt with fervent heat; both the earth and the works that are in it will be burned up. Therefore, since all these things will be dissolved, what manner of persons ought you to be in holy conduct and godliness, looking for and hastening the coming of the day of God, because of which the heavens will be dissolved, being on fire, and the elements will melt with fervent heat?" 2 Peter 3:10-12.

"I must work the works of Him who sent Me while it is day; the night is coming when no one can work," John 9:4.

"Therefore, as we have opportunity, let us do good to all, especially to those who are of the household of faith," Galatians 6:10.

When you have salvation, you have the Holy Spirit, deliverance, gifts, Fruit of the Spirit, battle armor, the Word of God, prayer, and the knowledge of the End Times. You have everything you need to live an abundant and prosperous life in Him. Your command is to love God and love people. When you chose to follow those two commands, amazing things will happen in your life. My prayer for you is that His grace and peace would abound to you that you might walk with Him in strength, power, hope, faith, and joy.

Stepping Stones

1. There are seven dispensations of time. We are in the sixth dispensation.

2. The rapture is the snatching away of those who have received the gift of salvation.

3. The Bema Judgment Seat of Christ judges the works of born-again believers.

4. The tribulation is seven years of God's wrath being poured out on the earth.

5. The Marriage Supper of the Lamb is a huge banquet to celebrate the Bride of Christ and the Lamb of God's union.

6. The Battle of Armageddon is a devastating war that occurs on earth.

7. Jesus comes again to earth in the second coming to take the devil captive.

8. The millennium is a thousand years of peace before the final rebellion.

9. The White Throne Judgment judges, rewards, and punishes all those who did not attend the Bema Judgment seat.

10. Jesus establishes the New Kingdom.

The End of – Well, Pretty Much Everything

Walking in Eternity

1. Do you or your church believe in pre-tribulation, mid-tribulation, or post-tribulation rapture? Why?

2. Which event judges the lives of believers: The Judgment Seat of Christ or the Great White Throne Judgment? What happens at this judgment?

3. Who will not experience the Rapture? Are these people doomed forever?

4. Who is the bride of Christ?

5. What can you do to ensure your place in the kingdom of God?

Glossary

SIMPLE GLOSSARY OF A FEW WORDS FROM THE CHRISTIAN FAITH

Adultery - The act of being sexually unfaithful to one's spouse

Agape - Affection, goodwill, love, brotherly love, a love feast

Angel - Messenger of God

Apostasy - Turning away from the religion, faith, or principles that one used to believe

Apostle - One sent forth, one chosen and sent with a special commission as a fully authorized representative of the sender.

Atonement - To cover, blot out, forgive; restore harmony between two individuals.

Attribute – An inherent characteristic

Backslide - To go back to ungodly ways of believing or acting.

Blasphemy - Words or actions showing a lack of respect for God or anything sacred.

Bless - To make or call holy, to ask God's favor, to praise; to make happy.

Blessing - A prayer asking God's favor for something, something that brings joy or comfort.

Born-again – To be begotten or birthed from God, the beginning, to start anew

Carnal - Of the flesh or body, not of the spirit, worldly; seat of one's desires opposed to the spirit of Christ

Cherubim - Guardian angels, angels that guard or protect places

Commitment - A promise, a pledge

Conditional - Placing restrictions, conditions, or provisions to receive

Conversion - Turn, return, turn back; change

Convert - To change from one form or use to another, to change from one belief or religion to another.

Courtship - The act or process of seeking the affection of one with the intent of seeking to win a pledge of marriage

Covenant - A pledge, alliance, agreement

Cult - A body of believers whose doctrine denies the deity of Christ.

Deliverance - A freeing or being freed, rescue; the act of change or transformation.

Demon - Evil spirit

Devil - Principal title for satan, the archenemy of God and man

Dispensation - A period of time, sometimes called ages

Dominion - To rule over, have power over, overcome, exercise lordship over

Eros - Erotic, physical love

Eternal - Existing always, forever, without time

Evangelist - Proclaims the gospel of Jesus Christ

Faith - Believing, trusting, depending, and relying on God

Fellowship - Sharing, communion, partnership, intimacy

Forgiveness - To pardon, release from bondage

Fornication - To act like a harlot, to be unfaithful to God, illicit sexual intercourse

Glorification - Salvation of the body, transforming mortal bodies to eternal bodies

Grace - Unmerited favor of God, help given in the time of need from a loving God

Holy - Set apart, sacred

Intercession - To meet or encounter, to strike upon, to pray for another

Justification - Salvation of the spirit, just as if I never sinned

Marriage - A divine institution designed by God as an intimate union, which is physical, emotional, intellectual, social, and most importantly, spiritual

New Testament - Text of the new covenant

Offering - Everything you give beyond your tithe

Old Testament - Text of the old covenant

Omnipotent - All-encompassing power of God

Omnipresent - Unlimited nature of God, ability to be everywhere at all times

Omniscient - God's power to know all things

Pastor - Shepherds of the body of believers

Philia - Conditional love, based on feelings, friendships

Praise - Thanksgiving, to say good things about, words that show approval.

Prayer - Communication with God

Prophet - One who is a spokesperson for God, one who has seen the message of God and declares that message

Propitiation - To satisfy the anger of God, to gain favor; appease

Rapture - To be carried away, or the catching away of

Reconciliation - Restore harmony or fellowship between individuals, to make friendly again

Redemption - To buy back, to purchase, recover, to Rescue from sin

Regeneration - To give new life or force to, renew, to be restored, to make better, improve or reform, to grow back anew

Repent - To give new life or force, to renew, to be restored, to make better, improve or reform, to grow back a new.

Resurrection - A return to life subsequent to death

Revelation - The act of revealing or making known

Righteousness - Right standing with God, integrity, virtue, purity of life, correctness of thinking

Sacrifice - The act of offering something, giving one thing for the sake of another; a loss of profit

Salvation - Deliverance from any kind of evil whether material or spiritual, being saved from danger or evil; to rescue.

Sanctification - Salvation of the soul. Separation from the seduction of sin

Satan - The chief of fallen spirits, opponent; adversary

Sealing - Something that guarantees, a sign or token, to make with a seal to make it official or genuine

Sin - All unrighteousness, missing the mark, wrong or fault; violation of the law

Spirit - A being that is not of this world, has no flesh or bones

Steward - A guardian or overseer of someone else's property, manager

Supernatural - Departing from what is usual, normal, or natural to give the appearance of transcending the laws of nature

Talent - A natural skill that is unusual.

Tithe - Ten percent of all your increase

Tribulation - Distress, trouble, a pressing together, pressure, affliction

Trinity - Three in one: Father, Son, Holy Spirit

Unconditional - No restrictions, conditions, boundaries, demands, or specific provisions

Will – Choice, inclination, desire, pleasure, command, what one wishes or determines shall be done

About the Author

Pamela is a teacher, mentor, and author of the inspirational book *Destiny Arise* and children's books including *Time in a Tuna*. Pam earned her bachelor's degree at the University of Illinois Springfield, her master's degree in Organizational Leadership at Lincoln Christian University, and her doctorate in Leadership at Christian Leadership University. She serves as a mentor for the Spirit Life Circles sponsored by CLU.

She works from her home in the prairie land of central Illinois. Pam and her bodybuilding husband own a gym/fitness center that promotes living a balanced life. She taught sixth grade for almost twenty years. Pam also taught preschool through adult-age students in various venues. She served as director of Super Church, the children's ministry in the United Methodist Church in her hometown. Pam also served in the church nursery, as director of New Life Ministries Discipleship Program, Vacation Bible School Director, Kingdom Kids Children's Ministry Director, and Sunday School teacher. She has also been on missionary trips. Her favorite trip, so far, was the time she spent in Belize.

Pam enjoys kayaking, bicycling, and riding her motor scooter. When she isn't writing, she enjoys spending time with her four children and their families which includes five grandchildren who are the inspiration of her children's books.

Walking with Jesus Series

BECOMING THE BEST ME I CAN BE

Book 1 - There Must Be a Better Way
Walking in Salvation

Book 2 - Lord, I Need Help!
Walking with the Holy Spirit

Book 3 - I Thought I Was Changed
Walking in Transformation

Book 4 - I Am Supernatural
Walking in Spiritual Gifts

Book 5 - I Am Strong
Walking as a Warrior

Book 6 - I Am Fruitful
Walking in the Fruit of the Spirit

Book 7 - Love Letters from God
Walking in the Word

Book 8 - Time in the Garden
Walking in the Power of Prayer

Book 9 - I'm in Charge of What?
Walking in Stewardship

Book 10 - The End of – Well, Pretty Much Everything
Walking into Eternity

Who am I? What am I doing here? Where am I going? Everyone at some point in life asks these questions. You were wired to ask and engineered to pursue the answers. The road to discovering destiny is besieged by fiascoes, failures, and the agony of defeat. If your strength has been depleted and has caused you to give up, sit down, push pause, and snooze until another day, then this book is just for you! Amazing experiences are waiting for you. Get ready to be awakened from the posture of defeat, depression, and despair.

Destiny Arise is an easy-to-read book, providing tools to aid in living an amazing life. This book is designed as a trip adviser for your expedition. It will teach you how to evict the spirit of mediocrity and use your past to propel you into your future. You will learn how to shake off the common, arising to be an uncommon force taking your rightful place in the earth. You can change the world. I pray this book will ignite a passionate fire to pursue your destiny unapologetically. Destiny, awake from your slumber and arise.

www.ingramcontent.com/pod-product-compliance
Lightning Source LLC
Chambersburg PA
CBHW062200100526
44589CB00014B/1892